# Keeping Track of Time

by Linda Kita-Bradley

Grass Roots Press

**Acknowledgements**

Grass Roots Press acknowledges the financial support of the Government of Canada for our publishing activities.

Canadä

Produced with the assistance of the Government of Alberta through the Alberta Media Fund.

Alberta

Editor: Dr. Pat Campbell
Photography: Susan Rogers
Book design: Lara Minja, Lime Design Inc.

**Library and Archives Canada Cataloguing in Publication**

Title: Keeping track of time / by Linda Kita-Bradley.

Names: Kita-Bradley, Linda, 1958- author.

Series: Kita-Bradley, Linda, 1958- Soft skills at work.

Description: Series statement: Soft skills at work

Identifiers: Canadiana 20200212141 | ISBN 9781771533447 (softcover)

Subjects: LCSH: Readers for new literates. | LCSH: Readers—Time management. | LCGFT: Readers (Publications)

Classification: LCC PE1126.N43 K58 2020 | DDC 428.6/2—dc23

# Part 1

Homer is a gardener.

Homer works at Pat's house.

Homer likes to talk.

Oh! Look at the time!

Pat has a big garden.

Pat says, "Look at the dry soil."

"Look at all the weeds."

Pat says, "The flowers need food."

"I want you to trim the bushes."

Homer thinks, "Where should I start?"

Homer likes to trim bushes.

But where is that trimmer?
It must be here!

Oh no!
Homer forgot to bring the trimmer.

So, he pulls some weeds.

Homer checks his phone for emails.

He feeds some flowers.

He pulls more weeds.

Oh! The soil is so dry!

Homer's phone rings.

Oh! Oh!
Homer is late for his next job.

Homer prays for rain.

Pat thinks, "What did Homer do today?"

# Talking About the Story

1. Imagine you are Pat. What do you say to Homer about his work?

2. Imagine you are Homer. Why do you have trouble keeping track of time?

3. Why is it important to keep track of time at work?

# Part 2

Read the next story about Homer and Pat.

How is it different from the first story?

Homer is a gardener.

He works at Pat's house.

Homer shows Pat his work plan.

They talk about the work plan.

Homer starts to pull weeds.
He pulls weeds by the path.

He pulls weeds by the rock garden.

Homer checks the time.
He needs to leave in two hours.

Homer pulls weeds in the lawn.
He pulls just the big weeds.

Homer gets the plant food.

He feeds the flowers.

Homer checks the time again.

His next job is the bushes.

But the soil is so dry!

Homer gets the hose.
He must water today.

Homer waters the garden.

Homer checks the time.

He has time to trim one bush.

Then he packs up for his next job.

Homer checks off the jobs on his plan.

He makes a note.

Pat is happy.
The garden looks great!

Manufactured by Amazon.ca
Bolton, ON